HOW TO CHANGE YOUR LIFE IN 7 STEPS

Want to improve your life but don't know where to start? Then this is the book for you.

In this highly-accessible self-help book, *Big Issue* founder John Bird explains his seven simple rules that could help you change your life.

Whether you want to get a new job, stop smoking, give up drinking or go back to college, *How to Change Your Life in 7 Steps* explains how you can take what you've been given and turn it into something you'll be proud of.

HOW TO CHANGE YOUR LIFE IN 7 STEPS

John Bird

BBC
LARGE
PRINT

First published in 2006 by
Vermilion, an imprint of Ebury
Publishing
This Large Print edition published in
2006 by BBC Audiobooks by
arrangement with Ebury Publishing
Random House UK Ltd

ISBN 1 4056 2188 5
ISBN 13: 978 1 405 62188 5

British Library Cataloguing in Publication Data available

Printed and bound by CPI Antony Rowe, Eastbourne

John Bird is the founder and editor of *The Big Issue*, a news and current affairs magazine launched in September 1991. It is written by professional journalists and sold on the streets by homeless vendors looking to break the cycle of poverty and homelessness. Vendors buy the magazine at a wholesale rate and sell it, keeping the profit for themselves. They are self-employed and encouraged to be responsible for handling their earnings.

John was born into a London Irish family in a slum-ridden part of Notting Hill just after the Second World War. Homeless at five, in an orphanage between seven and ten, he began to fail over and over again in every area of his life. From the age of ten onwards he was shoplifting, house-breaking and generally stealing whatever he could lay his hands on. Vandalism and arson were also among the crimes he committed.

In his late twenties, and after several prison sentences, John became involved in politics. He also fathered three children, became a printer, and successfully ran his own small business. At the age of 45, his many life experiences enabled him to start production of The Big Issue.

He has spent the last 14 years in charge of the development of *The Big Issue*—which is now an international movement—providing opportunities for people facing homelessness to help themselves. It forges partnerships with social entrepreneurs to launch businesses for social change in cities worldwide. Setting up street papers to help socially excluded people is central to this. People from all walks of life, from government ministers to prison inmates, are always asking him about what drove him so hard to make such a success of his life.

John Bird was awarded the MBE for 'services to homeless people' by Her Majesty the Queen in June 1995. He is a Fellow of John Moore's University, Liverpool, a Visiting Professor at Lincoln University, and a Doctor of Letters at Oxford Brookes University. In 2003, he was chosen by the Queen as one of the top Most Important Pioneers in Her Majesty's Reign. In 2004 he received from the United Nations a Scroll of Excellence for his international work in poverty, presented by the President of Kenya at the Habitat Celebration in Nairobi. In the same year he also won a public vote by BBC London as London's Living Legend, beating people such as Terence Conran, Barbara Windsor and Linford Christie.

Contents

Introduction

The trouble with aiming for the stars is that you can easily end up in the gutter. Don't get me wrong. I love the idea of aiming high, I really do. But I know from my own life that big ideas can often lead to a big fat nothing. That's because big can be scary. For many of us, just the thought of starting a new course, changing jobs or moving house is enough of a challenge. Doing it is another story.

So how do all those other people do it? How do they get things done—and make it look easy in the process? The answer is they think small. I'm not saying they don't have grand plans. They do. But instead of thinking about the end result, they set themselves modest targets, targets they can achieve easily. I call it starting with 3%. If you are sitting there wondering how to measure 3%, don't bother. I use the term 3% because it is a way of describing your first goal; a goal that you feel pretty sure of achieving. By sticking to it and building up slowly, you will move towards your goal. It's all about not setting yourself up to fail by taking on too much.

A friend and I once decided that we would write a book about Britain in the Victorian Age. We put our heads together and spent a lot of time talking about it. We got very excited. We kept talking about the book, but those talks did not include breaking it down into chapters. That was our first mistake. Instead, we kept planning and re-planning it, obsessed by our grand vision. Not long ago I went into my loft and found the book that my friend and I wrote some 25 years ago. I was really surprised at how good parts of it were. It could have really been something. But because we wanted to start with 100%, we ended up with nothing.

Quite often, the people who succeed are not even aware of their final goal. Once, when I was about 22 and on the run from the police, I got a job selling magazines to the public. It was a student magazine—or at least it was sold by people who said they were students. I had to go to this little basement flat and buy magazines from a young bloke who had started the magazine and had people selling it all over London. It was a great idea. The magazine was good, very good. The young bloke was keen, kind and very smart. He had got the magazine printed and he had published it. He had got it out into the streets. I still don't think I have ever seen such a serious magazine made for young people. Its most famous cover was of a young man with a large bulge in the front. The article was about what it would be like to be pregnant. It really

3

grabbed you. The magazine did not last too long, but the young bloke in the basement did. Next, he started a record business by mail. Then he got a shop. After that he started up all sorts of small businesses. Eventually that lad grew up and today he's a very well-known businessman— Richard Branson.

When Branson started Virgin he did not sit there and think, 'I want to start an empire.' He actually started by creating businesses, and as he realised what he could achieve, everything got bigger and bigger. Even today, he doesn't run his Virgin Group like one big business. The group is made up of lots of smaller businesses so it is easier to manage. Today, Branson's empire includes Virgin Atlantic, Virgin Trains, Virgin Money and his music Megastores, as well as many other businesses, all managed separately. Branson realises the need to think small as well as big.

From a small shop down a lane in Brighton, my friends Anita and Gordon Roddick started what was to become the massive Body Shop chain. The idea of the Body Shop was to make beauty products that did not harm animals and also helped suppliers in poorer countries. In the very early days the first containers for their products were those funny little bottles that doctors use for urine samples. The Roddicks were the first people to make many of us aware of exactly what went into the products we used, and of their effects on the planet. The Body Shop has since inspired a lot of other people to create companies with the same basic aims.

These, and many other stories like them, should remind us not to start by wanting to go too fast. The reason many good ideas do not see the light of day is that, unlike Branson and the Roddicks, we let ourselves get snowed under by the big idea. Then we get worn out because we think and worry about what we're trying to do, instead of taking the small steps that will help us achieve it.

1 START WITH 3%

Perhaps the best way for me to explain the value of my 3% rule is shown by the following story. At 15, I was caught and sent back to the institution I had run away from. My punishment was to dig over a huge space in a walled garden. I had to dig it with a spade, and then break it down with a pitchfork. Then the couch grass roots had to be bundled together and burnt. The size of the area I had to tackle would have made the strongest man cry. It was several weeks' worth of careful digging, forking and picking.

This was beyond the usual punishment. It was a method of torture that I knew they hoped would lead to me failing. They knew it would make me want to run away again. And if that happened I would be in even more trouble. And there might be no way back for me. Even at that age I knew this was a major turning point.

There was no way I could let this task beat me. For the first hour I did something very simple. I divided the ground into squares. That way it looked easier to manage. Working square by square, I would be able to see that I had achieved something and I could measure the amount of work I had done. Knowing that I was getting somewhere would keep me going. The warden came back and watched me as I measured the ground. He shouted at me and asked me what I was doing. I stood to attention and told him. He was speechless, and left!

In the weeks that followed I re-marked the squares so the lines would not fade. I could do two squares between the start of work and the midday break. Sometimes if I worked a bit faster I could get two-and-a-half squares done. I was pleased with myself. I did not let the big piece of ground grind me down. I just took it slowly and, each day, the task became smaller. Sure I may have been crawling along, but the main thing was that it was happening. By breaking down the job into smaller jobs, I had control over it. There is no great mystery to how I did it. I set myself a goal that I could live up to. I started with 3%. Each time I finished a square I added to that 3%. That meant that I was doing the job and I wasn't wearing myself out. I did not set myself up to fail and I showed the staff that I wasn't going to be broken by their punishment. But most importantly, I showed myself.

The despair of depression

There have been times in my life when I have felt truly lost, not just unhappy, but truly out of step with the world. You know those periods when you seem to have a dark cloud following you around, a cloud so heavy it doesn't even allow you to perform the simplest of tasks. You can't find any joy in anything. In fact, just being human is a struggle.

One time I was living on hand-outs from friends and a bit of social security money. Life was grim and there wasn't much reason to get out of bed. But if I wanted to break the pattern I had to start somewhere. So I set myself the smallest of tasks. First I praised myself for getting out of bed. Then I was pleased when I could brush my teeth each morning. (If you've ever been depressed, you'll understand exactly the effort this takes.) The fact that I added shaving to my daily routine was a major step. OK, it might sound stupid but I had to start somewhere. If I had woken up thinking of everything that I needed to do, I would never have got out of bed. Eventually I got to the stage where I could go out and look for a job.

I take exactly the same approach with the homeless. I always tell my employees that you can't expect too much from people who live on the streets. After all, in many cases they have never known a time when things were different so it is natural for them to feel that nothing will ever change. Asking too much of them is just setting them (and you) up to fail. So we don't. Instead we ask them to give us 3%. Just turning up on a regular basis is a huge step for homeless people. Once they've managed that, they are in a position to sell *The Big Issue*. Then we begin to expect more from them. The next time we see them we ask for 5%. We might say, 'Can you comb your hair before you turn up?' And so it goes. Eventually we expect them to give us 50% and we give them 50%. So they give as much as they take. And likewise we give them only what they need to stand on their own two feet.

Remember—one small step at a time

Watching homeless people change their lives is a joy. It is fantastic seeing people pull themselves out of the gutter. And it happens because we don't steam in asking for the world and pushing them to make big changes in their lives. If we did that, we would get nowhere.

Sometimes nothing happens because people will not accept the thought of starting with 3%. In my position, people come to me with big projects all the time. They want to change the face of society. They want to bring about social justice for everyone and nothing less will do. But when you ask how they'll do it, their plan falls to pieces because they want 100% or nothing. Guess what they end up with. Having dreams is wonderful, but you can't change the world simply because you want to. And we all know Rome wasn't built in a day.

Think back to something you tried to achieve in your life. What happened once you decided on a goal for yourself? I bet that you got excited for a couple of days and then, maybe a week later, you found the study/exercise/savings plan far too difficult. It is likely, too, that even the thought of doing the task was enough to wear you out. Suddenly you had all sorts of excuses as to why you couldn't go for that particular goal. I will also bet that it has happened to you more than once. I call this the 'all start and no finish' problem. You can get started but once things get going you lose your resolve and give up.

- So next time you want to make something happen in your life try this: set a goal you can achieve. What I mean is that you need a goal that doesn't rely on luck, or chance, or anybody else coming through for you. It has to be real, and not pie-in-the-sky stuff. That doesn't mean it has to be small. Just make sure it's within your grasp.

- Create a series of steps to help you get there. Set yourself up to succeed by making sure you are not trying to do too much, too quickly. Remember you only have to start with 3%. It doesn't matter if you move slowly. As long as you are not standing completely still you are on your way.
- Move the steps around if necessary to take account of life's changes. It is quite likely that work or family issues will disrupt your evening course, or your plans will veer off course. That is OK—just change your goal to include things that crop up. But be strict with yourself.
- Enjoy and celebrate your gains no matter how small. You went walking for 20 minutes? Great.

Don't worry that your best mate went running for an hour. It is *your* goal that matters—and *your* life. Allow yourself to take pleasure in the small steps you achieve. If others say, 'Well done,' be happy. Don't bring yourself down by saying things like, 'Well, it's not much.' It is more than you were doing before, so relish it. But don't be tempted to ease up.

And finally, remember—aim big, get there small.

2 STOP THINKING LIKE A VICTIM

The world is full of victims. I don't mean the millions who've suffered through war and conflict or injustice. I mean the weak, small-minded people who think their problems have nothing to do with them and everything to do with a world that is unfair. That's bad enough. But now being a victim has even become something to be proud of, to share with other people and display like a badge of honour.

If you are not sure what I'm talking about, then have a look at what I've written below and ask yourself if any of these points applies to you:

- You want others to know that you have had a bad time.
- You think everything that

happens to you is 'unfair'.

- You believe it is always other people who get the breaks.
- You secretly feel pleased when others feel sorry for you.
- You see the world through the eyes of defeat.

If you can identify with at least one of these, you join a growing group of people who think that being a victim is no bad thing. And telling the world about it is even better, especially if your life is pretty good now. Tony Blair jumped on the bandwagon when he told us how, as a youngster who wanted to form a band, he slept on the streets of London for a whole night. What a bloke! What a victim!

If you can identify with most of those points, my guess is that you are one of those people who believe the world is out to get you. You're at the mercy of everything: the banks/junk food/mad cows/ barking dogs/people who steal your parking spot. The media love people like you. TV shows like *Jerry Springer*, *Richard and Judy*, and *Trisha*, all devote a large amount of time to people telling us how bloody awful their lives are.

The blame culture

It's always the fault of someone else that their boyfriend/girlfriend/ wife/ husband left them. Somebody else made them overweight. The doctor forced them to become addicted to sleeping pills. And then the media steps in and eggs these people on and invents even more ways for people to become victims. Picked the wrong holiday? Go on TV and blame the holiday company. Paid too much for insurance? Don't worry, there's someone you can tell your story to and drum up some sympathy.

The media, and the stupid people who play along with them, present 'normal' life as never having problems, obstacles or arguments.

The truth is that life is actually about overcoming those to get the things you want. It is not easy and it is often not fair. But who said the world had to be? Whoever said that life had to go your way? The fact is that even when you bust a gut trying to do your best, it still might not go your way. Because that's just how things are.

I'm not saying that these people haven't suffered or felt pain. My point is that what they have gone through is perfectly normal and should be expected as part of life. But because they have chosen to take a certain view of the world, they believe that what has happened to them has nothing to do with their own actions. And like all victims, they believe that the world revolves around them.

One of the things you notice about victims is that they don't care about anybody else. They are always ready to tell you how much harder their life is. My daughter was working in a very stressful job. She was new at it and she was finding it a bit of a struggle. Looking for advice, she went to speak to her line manager about how difficult she was finding things. Her manager, a man who had done very well, could only respond by telling her how much harder he'd had it in his career. He did not bother to listen to her. She wasn't looking to compare jobs with this man, she was looking for support. But he was too wrapped up in himself to see it.

The world may screw you up—but you have to sort yourself out

At the other end of the scale, but not really much different, is Norman. Norman has self-pity written all over him. He is the ultimate victim. He is overweight because he only eats sweet stuff. When he sells *The Big Issue* he sits down even though he is not supposed to. He smokes until he can hardly breathe. And he gets very angry with the world. He reckons that everyone else has all the breaks. He missed out and there is nothing left for him. He wants to be a writer. He sees all the bad books being written. He tries reading some of them. But they are so rubbish there is no way he would ever want to finish them. You know those books you find in an airport shop? Norman picks them up and wants to fling them down because they are so bad. The books annoy him so much they make his life even worse. After reading them he can't write.

Norman has reasons to be bitter and sad. We all have. How many times have you felt sorry for yourself because you missed out on the job/the house/the boyfriend you deserved? I'll bet you thought you were the only one in the whole world who never got what they wanted. But let me ask you this: did you really go after it?

Pat's story

In my work with the homeless I meet many Normans. But I also meet people like Pat. The difference between them is a thousand miles, or so it would seem. Pat is a small man in his late forties. He came to work with me about five years ago. When he arrived he had already decided that he wanted to work with the staff who deal with all our *Big Issue* sellers.

That's a tough job. It means putting up with the complaints, the moans, the anger and the self-pity of the homeless. Why someone would want to stay in the firing line for five years beats me. I have to say I do not have the patience of a Pat. But every day there he was, taking stick from people who wanted to blame anyone around for their problems. Pat was a quiet bloke. But it soon became obvious that he knew how to handle a crisis. He knew how to restore calm and stop people getting violent.

Pat himself had been homeless once. He had slept on the streets. He had been a drinker. He had even been a fighter. But then he had stopped it all. One night he told me what had changed his mind about being a 'waster' (the word he used to describe himself).

'I remember you coming into the depot one night. About eight years ago. You were in a bad mood. I had been pissing everyone off. I think you wanted to throw me out.'

I didn't remember the incident. But suddenly I recognised Pat from those years as a *Big Issue* seller, but not as the calm, controlled Pat who sat in front of me. 'Back then,' he carried on, 'you said, "There's a drunk outside. Someone should sort him out else he'll get arrested."' I still didn't remember it. 'Anyway I went out and helped the drunken bloke. I got him sobered up. I got him a place to sleep at Waterloo.' Pat then told the story of a year that changed his life. My simple comment that someone should help the drunk had been a turning point. He had started to help others. 'I realised that as long as I saw myself as a victim, I would always be one.'

Having helped just one man, Pat realised how good it felt to turn all that bad energy into something useful. He stopped thinking about his own problems. As often happens with people who help others, he found something inside himself that had been missing all these years: self-esteem. And the more he began to work and help others, the more that self-esteem grew. Pat did not need to be a noisy, violent drunk any more to prove himself. He simply had to keep doing what made him feel good about himself. And he did it without making any huge changes. As I said at the start of this book, you only need to start with 3%.

The other lesson I think we can all learn from Pat is that he found something that made him feel good. If you are stuck in a job you hate or a relationship that isn't working, you are more likely to think and act like a victim. You need to take control of your life and feel that you, not anybody else, is in charge.

Stop making excuses
I was worse than Pat: I used to set myself up to be a victim. I would smash a door in at a party, pick on a bunch of 'suits', or get drunk and go joy-riding, just waiting for the police to come after me. Once I arrived drunk at a party, took a bottle of wine and broke the top on the side of a table. I poured the contents down my throat. I was then restrained by two blokes. I knocked one to the floor. The other ran off and I sat down and cried about how terrible my life had been. I always had my past waiting in the wings in case I needed an excuse.

One of the hardest things is to stop

making excuses to yourself and others. I can't tell you how many reasons I've found for not writing the chapters in this book. I meant to write them but something always got in the way. Having a new baby gave me one of the best excuses I'd had for weeks. When I couldn't come up with any more, I knew I had to knuckle down. Otherwise the book would never get written.

Working with the homeless means I hear loads of excuses. 'But John, I've only been off the streets for two years.' Two years later they are telling me they've only been off the streets for four years. And so on. When I suggest a course of action they usually say something like, 'It's all right for you.' They always have an answer, but it is never a good one.

You might think that making an excuse puts you in control of your life, but actually it shows the opposite: that you are not able to get your act together. Excuses are a way of not facing up to reality. They are yet another weapon for victims to pull out when things get a bit difficult, another way of saying, 'feel sorry for me'. But they are a habit that you can break. Next time you find yourself making an excuse, ask yourself how you would feel if someone gave that excuse to you. 'I broke my diet and ate the entire pack of chocolate biscuits because there was nothing else in the house.' 'I am staying in my relationship because I won't find another one.' Do you really want to know that person?

Stop feeling sorry for yourself
Pat and I both learned something in our lives that I hope will become obvious to you: the more you feel sorry for yourself, the worse your life gets. I call it the circle of pity, and the bigger it gets the harder it is to get out of. How much have you done to feed your circle of pity? If you

answered 'yes' to most of the points at the beginning of this chapter then you are feeding it four-course meals on a regular basis. As soon as we start feeling sorry for ourselves we make sure there is no room for change in our lives. Even if you are given the biggest chance in the world, you will not see it if you are wrapped up in self-pity.

It's easy to remain a sad bastard. I know because I was one. Right up until my forties, I let all those years of neglect and childhood abuse dominate my life. It took me years to throw off my victim mentality because it took me years to realise how damaging it was. But I did it. And you can too.

What doesn't kill you makes you stronger

Even today I still look back and think, 'Bloody hell, Johnny, you did it.' There are some things I've learned that might help you begin. I am not expecting you to make big changes all of a sudden. The whole point of starting with 3% is that it allows you to make small changes that you can build on at your own pace.

• Give yourself a new label
People who think in a positive way believe that you become what you think you are. If you think you are a self-pitying, drunk bastard, then you will stay one. If you think you are the ugly best friend, then you will continue to be. These are all the sorts of labels that victims give themselves. Today is the day you give yourself the label for what you want to become. Slim career girl? Thoughtful dad?

• Get rid of destructive behaviour
This includes removing yourself from friends and others who aren't going to help. I am not saying wipe out your current life. But think about

how you can be around people who support you. Anyone who does any sort of class, for example, is bound to be interested in improving themselves. These are good people to be around. In my case I had to stop drinking and fighting. It didn't happen overnight. But it did happen.

• Act instead of talking about it
Remember, no more excuses. I know this won't be easy, but here's a tip: next time you find yourself about to complain to your best friend yet again about your relationship, change the subject. Do not even allow her to ask about it. Just say you're working on it. Then go off and work on it. I went through a lot of twists and turns to get *The Big Issue* off the ground, but I stuck with it. I just kept adding that 3% on gradually.

• Don't compare yourself to others
These days I am lucky to know lots

of clever, successful and wealthy people. I admire them but I don't go around wishing I was them. Don't measure yourself by the deeds of celebrities, neighbours or even members of your own family. Why waste your valuable time worrying about what others have got? Just focus on your own life and your own goals, no matter how small they may be. That way you'll have more energy to build the life you want.

• Make the best of the worst
Anybody can make the best of the best times in life, but the real trick is to make the best of the worst times. If you look at successful people in life, you might find something very interesting—that a lot of them made their own breaks. And they often began their 'successful' life when something had gone wrong for them. They never thought about being victims. Instead they used a time of great personal change as an

opportunity to reinvent their lives. Like a woman I know—when she was 42, her husband left her and her three children with no money. She did not let it defeat her. Eventually she started her own recruitment company and became very successful. Never once did it occur to her that she was a victim. She knew she was an adult with a choice. And so are you.

*   *   *

So do you let self-pity take hold of your life and ruin any chances you have for happiness? Or do you get up and take that victim badge off now?

You are no longer a victim if:
- You do not believe the world owes you a living.
- You know you have to go through thorns to find roses.
- You refuse to hang around with

victims.
- You know the grass is not always greener on the other side.
- You refuse to use your past as an excuse.
- You take setbacks as an opportunity to gain strength.
- You spend more time thinking about others.
- You replace excuses with action.

3 BE TRUE TO YOURSELF AND OTHERS

We know the world is full of liars. We know that when an estate agent describes a house as 'quaint' it is really a heap of shit. And that when your company says they are going to 'streamline' things you are probably about to lose your job. We know that banks spend millions of pounds making ads to convince us that they are acting on our behalf, while they continue to act in their own interests. Some lies can help life run smoothly: 'Of course I'll make a payment tomorrow.' And some lies are just part of life. Where would schoolchildren be without, 'The dog ate my homework'?

Then there are the lies that have become part of our lives but shouldn't. The news is full of business leaders and politicians who talk a lot while stretching the truth. Tony Blair and his cabinet ministers told us there were weapons of mass destruction in Iraq so often that they started to believe the lie. But they have made it harder for us to believe them next time.

In a society like this, why should we bother telling the truth? The answer is that if we do, people know where we stand. And they are more likely to listen to our opinions. Because telling lies robs us of other qualities. It takes away trust and respect, and without those we don't have very much.

I used to tell people that I lied and cheated 'on behalf of the homeless'. My reason for this was that I had decided the world ran on lies of one sort or another. Since I couldn't beat the bastards, I might as well join them. The poor needed someone who was using the system for their benefit. And I had a good reason to keep doing what I had done for most of my life. I never for one moment thought that the lies I told other people were lies to myself. But that's exactly what they were. I used them to create a kind of false universe so that I did not have to face up to the life I had. I did not have much, but lying meant I lost even that. And in one of life's twists, I learned that the less you have, the more you need the truth.

Lying feels good—until you get found out

Once when I was in youth prison, we were painting a wall. As we painted we talked and this bloke asked me who I was and where I came from. He asked me what my father did for a living. Without missing a beat I told him that my father was an architect and had built a city called Brasilia which happens to be the capital of Brazil. I told him about all the hard work my father had to do to get the city running, and all the roads that he had to build to get to the new city. The boy was very interested. And since I knew a lot about the city of Brasilia I was able to give loads of detail.

One of the officers was listening in. When I had finished he came over. 'Your dad's an architect, Bird?' I saluted him. 'Yes sir.' He then stroked his head as if he was struggling with an idea. 'Funny, I thought your dad was a builder's labourer from Fulham Broadway.' I shrank, and tried to protest. But it didn't work. And the thing was if you were shown to be a liar then soon enough everyone would know about it. I lost some ground that day. And the funny thing was that even though I was in youth prison, where there was no shortage of liars and thieves, that lie still stood out.

I kept on telling lies. It was a habit. I told my first wife that she had met an eighteen-year-old aristocrat by the name of Jonathan Delarue. I told her I was the black sheep of a very rich family. It was one of my longest-running lies and lasted for over six months. Until the day I had to tell her the truth and I took her to a block of council flats in Fulham to meet the Irish office cleaner who was my Mum.

The lies went on for a long time. Reading about it now may seem funny, but behind those lies was an attempt to be somebody. I see it in the homeless people I work with. I can't tell you how many dramatic stories I've heard from people trying to justify why they were on the street. You'd hear things like, 'My wife and three children were burned to death in a house fire. I survived and after that I was too messed up to work. I got depressed, lost everything, turned to alcohol and here I am.' When you did get the truth out of them you'd find out that they stopped going to work because they couldn't be bothered, or they were caught stealing and got fired. Even though they were at the bottom of the pile, they wanted me to think they led more interesting lives.

Lying can even be dangerous ...

I used to run a youth group around Shepherds Bush. Every Friday night we had a disco in a council hall. The council wanted us to have the disco because of all the youngsters who were hanging around doing nothing. The first night seemed to be going well. I met a young, fit-looking lad. He was always bobbing around throwing punches that stopped just an inch from your face, but it didn't annoy me. He boxed for a local club and he looked and talked as though he knew how to handle himself. He talked pretty big. I was getting sick of the talk so I thought I had better give him something to do. I told him to take up a position by the door and not to let anyone in without a ticket. I figured he could handle it.

As I walked across the floor I suddenly saw a horrible sight. A boy had pulled a knife out and had it poised over the back of another boy. I jumped sideways and grabbed the hand with the knife.

The shout went up. 'Bundle!' meaning fight. And suddenly boys from the street who didn't have a ticket poured in. It became a mass fight. Windows were broken. The police were there within minutes. The boy who had tried to stab the other boy had gone, and I had the knife. When things calmed down I looked for the boxer, as we called him, but he had also disappeared. He hadn't stopped the boys coming in and starting the brawl. Later, I met the boxer and had a word with him. I could tell that all that bouncing around and throwing punches was cover. He was trying to cover up the fact that he wasn't the hard person he wanted to be. He had lied about himself—and it could have been fatal.

Truth leads to freedom
One of the films I really love is *Being There*. The book and the film are so simple and beautiful. The leading role in the film is played by Peter Sellers. His character, Chauncey Gardiner, cannot lie. He has lived in a house with an old man all his life. He is a simple person whom the old man has tried to protect from the world. You might call him a bit slow. When the old man dies Chauncey has to leave the only life he has ever known. He knows nothing else except his garden and what he has seen on TV.

Chauncey's child-like innocence makes a huge impact on everyone he comes into contact with. He has worked in the garden of the old man for so long that he only knows the world of the grass and the trees and the flowers. When anyone asks him a question, he answers very simply. But people see him as being very wise, and soon his words of wisdom are even being listened to by the President of the United States, who is sick of all the other stuff he hears. It's a clever film because on the one hand you could say that Chauncey is fooling all these people who are meant to be smart. But you could also argue that in a world full of lies, spin and half-truths, people want to believe in something that is more pure. They like Chauncey because he seems so innocent. And, unlike them, he is free.

There is a saying that 'the truth sets you free'. Believe me, it does. It was only when I stopped lying to myself and to other people, at the ripe old age of 45, that I was able to move on and make something of myself. But it wasn't just the outright lies. All those years of excuses and broken promises had not helped me either. They just tied me up in knots.

Keeping promises is a very

powerful form of telling the truth. If you say you'll do something, do it. If you promise you'll show up, be there. If you say you'll deliver high quality, don't skimp. If you can't do it, then don't make up excuses. Be honest and explain to people why. They will respect you for your honesty. They might still be annoyed, but at least they will know you are an honest person.

Now I am not saying this is easy. If you've spent most of your life hiding behind lies and creating a pretend version of yourself, then it's going to be even harder. And then of course there is the thought of hurting others or looking stupid. But the other side of the coin is the way that lies shut you in your own personal prison and stop you from living your life.

It is normal not to tell people what is really going on in your life because you are afraid of looking weak, difficult or stupid. But it means you are just putting things off. If you tell the truth, people have a chance to find out about problems while there's still time to do something about them. Telling the truth enables the truth to be dealt with in a positive way. If the other person doesn't want to listen to you, *you've* found out the truth about *them.* Then you can decide whether you want to keep up the relationship or not. And you can move on. You are free of something that wasn't working. But if you don't tell the truth, how will you ever know?

*   *   *

Of all the chapters in this book, putting this one into practice is probably the hardest. This is because:
- All human beings tell lies.
- Lies are a part of our lives.
- Lies can make life flow more easily for a while.
- Lies can be more fun (for a bit).

- Lies can help you convince yourself your life is not that bad.
- Lies give you something to hide behind.
- Lies help you put off the rest of your life.

All these are true, but all very short term. And if you are reading this book then chances are you want to be here for a long time. So here are some reasons why the truth will help you.

- 'If you tell the truth you do not have to remember anything.' (Mark Twain)
- There is no need to remember to keep your stories straight as your stories are facts, so less effort is required.
- When you stick to what you know is right or wrong, you don't regret anything you have done.
- Other people will follow your example and act more honestly.
- People are more likely to listen

to your opinions and ideas. This means that you have more chance of being promoted at work, etc.

- If you get a reputation as someone who tells it like it is, people are less likely to try and put one over on you.
- It is easier for you to figure out who to trust.
- You will handle rejection and criticism more easily.
- You will have fewer clashes of personality with others.

4 STOP KNOCKING EVERYONE ELSE

In Australia there's something called the 'Tall Poppy Syndrome'. It refers to the national habit of knocking down anyone who has any status, shows any hint of being too clever or has success. It doesn't just happen in Australia of course. Knocking people who achieve happens everywhere. In early 2005, Tesco, Britain's largest grocer, announced a 5% profit margin. You'd think the business writers would have been happy with such news. Instead, many of them called for something to be done to 'cut them down to size'. But even if Tesco had done badly, those people wouldn't have been happy.

Look at the reaction to Bob Geldof's Live 8 concerts and the entire Make Poverty History movement. The cynics had a field day, throwing everything they could at Geldof and co. They didn't stop and think about what he was trying to do. It didn't enter their heads that he was trying to find a way of making the public aware of poverty in Africa where others had not been able to. Instead they picked at the motives of Geldof and the others who had joined him. Not for one moment was there the thought that he was putting his neck on the line.

Jamie Oliver is another high-profile example of somebody who has attracted more than his fair share of knocks from other people. Maybe you are one of them. The lad has put his heart and soul into his projects and he certainly hasn't taken the easy route. Anyone who tells you that Jamie does it simply for publicity ignores the facts. In his own small way, he's revived the idea of being an apprentice, and of the work spirit. He recently started focusing on school dinners, where he stuck himself right in it by trying to cook wholesome food for a very small amount of money. He didn't say, 'Oh, I can't do it because I need £1.50 for each child. All I've got is a third of that.' He just got on and did it anyway. Jamie's efforts have led to other people wanting to work with him.

These days, knocking others has become an industry. Our newspapers employ people whose main task is to write columns telling us what's wrong with the world. Those who practise knocking on a regular basis would argue that what they do stops people getting above themselves. Half bully and half party-pooper, the knocker is always looking for the bad and the ugly. And they don't stop at the rich and powerful. Everybody and everything is a target. For people who think this way, everything always has a downside and very little upside. Even an outright success is not a success. I am thinking of a newspaper article that described a sporting team's win as 'not a good win'. What rubbish! This kind of pickiness shows how far the knocking industry has invaded our society. Nothing seems to be good enough anymore.

I sit in a café writing this. Near me are two women who are chatting very loudly. They are complaining, firstly about the phone company they are using, then about their banks. And then they launch into a whole list of other things. I suddenly realise that if you took complaints out of people's lives there wouldn't be much left. It's in our nature to want to have a moan. And sometimes it does you good to let it all out. But when those complaints become a big part of your conversation and when they start including things you can't control, you are heading down a very tricky path.

Put your energy to better use
It would be better by far to be using that energy to change the things you don't like, but you won't if you spend your life listening to the knockers. Like poison, their views will affect the way you think. Instead of thinking all things are possible, you'll be telling yourself that it is too hard. Before you've even dipped a toe into the water and tried something new, you'll have given up.

I understand how tempting it is to join the knocking brigade. It's a chance to air your views and even be a bit clever without actually having to do anything else. And it's a way of telling yourself you are above it all, and that you could do those things if you wanted to but you've chosen not to. We're all guilty of it, but if you do it on a regular basis then you'll eventually find it very hard to make changes in your life. To be able to make these changes you need a more positive outlook. So to make a start you have to control the negative thoughts you have about others. I'm not saying you shouldn't have a friendly little moan with your mates at the pub. What I am saying is don't turn it into a lifetime habit. It's a well-known fact that knockers have never changed anything worth changing.

Me, on the receiving end

One very cold wet night I went round to a friend's house. I did not want to go, but I had cancelled on him twice before and didn't want to let him down. The streets were full of rubbish bags blowing about and flying roof tiles. It was a bad night to be out. My friend was in a strange mood. He sat there smoking, drinking and looking at me. Having made rude comments on my repeated failure to turn up, he then decided to rubbish everything I had ever done. He had known me since childhood so he knew all about my past. He decided that my work with the homeless was just another of my cunning schemes and there was no way I could make any real change anyway. Partly out of shock I just sat, drank tea and listened.

As I left his flat I felt I had witnessed something that I needed to think about more. He had shown me the pain and bitterness of what it was like to sit on the sidelines and shoot arrows at people who were trying to change either their own lives or the lives of others.

Soon after that I had to deal with those arrows in a more public way. *The Big Issue* had run into financial problems with a fall in advertising. We had to slim the company down. A company like *The Big Issue* depends on the marketplace. We are not a charity and cannot appeal for more money from the public. Often the downsizing of a business brings out all the gripes within the organisation.

Sure enough it all came to the

surface. A particular person left *The Big Issue* on a Friday and on the following Monday made a vicious, bitter attack on me and my leadership in the press. In that person's eyes, I was the destroyer of *The Big Issue*. Suddenly John Bird, the one-time saint and saviour of the homeless, was mud. Luckily, the damage was limited. But that day I learned just how many people are out there waiting for you to fail. I also learned that you have to do your best not to take any notice of them.

The reason my friend had turned on me that evening was, I believe, because he hated his own inactivity. He seemed to have spent his life believing that things could not work. He rubbished all my attempts. And, yes, maybe he even envied me. How many of your opinions are a result of that kind of envy?

People don't like facing up to change

Knockers come in some unexpected disguises. Sometimes even the people closest to you will make it difficult for you to succeed. Have you ever told your family and friends your latest plans and found their response lukewarm? You tell them you plan to spend a year overseas, but instead of being excited for you, they point out the problems they are sure you are going to have. You'll be alone, they say. You won't make friends. You don't speak the language. What if you're robbed? Or even worse? Don't be too surprised by all this. It's likely that they just don't understand what you are doing and therefore find it hard to support you. Most people fear change, so if somebody close to them makes a move, it forces them to think about their own lives when they don't want to.

The story of the overweight

woman who wants to slim down but is told by her friends, 'Oh, you don't need to, we love you exactly as you are,' shows the sneaky tactics people will use to keep you where you are. The reason they don't want her to lose weight is that it will change her as a person and it may very well change their friendship. To stop that happening her friends try to scupper her efforts. They are not nasty people, but they are afraid.

Try to find sources of genuine support

To stop your own efforts being destroyed, you need to make sure you spend more time with people who want you to succeed and be happy in your life. That might sound harsh, but I am thinking you bought this book with the intention of getting your life on track. So don't hang around with people who want to throw you off it, no matter how well-meaning they are.

Let me be clear that I am not talking about people who offer intelligent, thoughtful views and ideas—they are always welcome in my house. But these days I refuse to be with people who can only point out the problems. If I had listened to the knockers, I would never have started *The Big Issue*. Let's face it, I was trying to get the homeless off the streets, something that governments and charities had tried to do over the years and never achieved. I'm not perfect by a long shot, but I know in my heart that when everyone else stood by and wrote off the homeless I made something happen.

Negative vibes in the workplace

Offices and places of work are classic breeding grounds for knockers. You are surrounded by people that you can have a go at and policies that you do not agree with. But the fact is that you have to go in there every day and do a job. Spending your day bitching about everything is not going to make it any more pleasant for you. Worse, you might find that people start avoiding you because they think you just whinge all the time. Most of us want our lives to be easier so, sooner or later we are going to fall out with anybody who creates an obstacle to that goal.

A woman who once worked for me was the most destructive person I have ever met. On the surface she was kind, friendly and lively. But she expected failure. Needless to say what she said often came to pass, which is no surprise if you work with homeless people. They will often fall down at some point. And when they do, they don't always get up quickly. It can annoy you and will push your patience to the limit. It also means you need to hire a special kind of person who can keep the ball in the air no matter how bad things are looking. This woman was not like that. She said all the right things, but deep within her she had a strong belief our ideas would not work. She should not have been working with people who felt so low about their lives, because despite her sunny appearance her outlook on life was no brighter than theirs.

She brought people down around her. She kept saying 'no' to things. She was a drain on our goodwill. Sure she did some good work, but her lack of belief in our way of doing things meant that there was no way that she would have helped move us forward. She could not improve us. She could only point out our problems. I was more patient then and believed that she could be reformed because she was smart. These days I wouldn't keep her around for longer than it takes to say 'see you later'. She was with us for two years. It was two years too long.

Is it a broken egg? Or an omelette?
Life is not perfect. Public transport is not perfect, the weather is not perfect and celebrities and politicians are far from perfect. Your boss, no matter who he or she is, will almost certainly never be perfect. If you are at least 20, you should have figured this out by now. And by reading this you should also have figured out that if you knock people and complain about things it will not get you very far towards your goals.

- Make the change you want to see. You have to get off your backside and get involved in the world and do something. Stop complaining about what doesn't work. Do something rather than blow hot air at everybody else. Look at yourself before you judge others.
- For every negative thought about someone else's actions, try and think how you would have done

it better. That way at least you will end up a positive being. You might even find it leads to a very good idea.

- Avoid hanging around with people who can't see the positives. This includes those well-meaning friends who don't want you to change because of their own inactivity. Don't make a song and dance about it. Just know that not all human beings reach the same stages at the same time—even your friends.

- The thought that you might fail should not stop you making an effort. And if you do fail, at least you tried, which is better than most people.

- Be an individual, with your own view of life. As long as the human race has existed, there has always been poverty, tragedy, violence and the great unknown. That has never stopped people before. It's only life after all.

- Remember knockers have never changed anything worth changing. Oscar Wilde said, 'A cynic knows the price of everything and the value of nothing.' A knocker knows the value of nothing and is not very good on the price.

5 THINK FOR YOURSELF

Does your mind belong to you? You are probably thinking, 'That's a bloody stupid question.' Actually it isn't. Lots of people act as if their minds belong to somebody else. They just drift along picking up a bit of knowledge from this person, an idea from that person. And so it goes. What they are doing is letting other people decide what their views are and how they should react to the world. They accept the values taught by their parents, teachers, religious figures, or friends, without question.

Owning your own mind is not always easy. We live in a world that wants us to conform and obey. It wants to tell us what to think. I am writing this a month after the London terrorist bombings. The papers are full of opinions about why people decide to become bombers. Many of the people who write these articles are convinced they are absolutely right and their tone suggests that we should agree with them.

In a world where we have information coming at us from all angles, it is often much easier and less tiring not to question what lies behind that information. But if you go through life accepting everything others tell you, you ignore one of your most valuable rights: the right to think for yourself. Having your own mind means that you, and only you, decide whether what you are being told by the newspapers and radio and TV makes sense. It means that you don't just accept what everybody tells you or let other people influence you any more than you want them to.

I'm not talking about being stubborn, quite the opposite in fact. Having your own mind is about being strong and free enough to decide things for yourself, and to resist the views of others. It also means being strong enough to make your own decisions and to stick by them, even if you make mistakes. After all, they are your own mistakes. I'm not saying you should reject what people tell you just to prove a point. That would be stupid. But you need to be able to think about what others say and not be afraid to question it.

Do you have the same political views as your parents or your partner or friend because you've never given any thought to what they believe in? Have you thought about what you believe in? If you have children, do you find yourself bringing them up in the same way your parents brought you up? Why?

I had a girlfriend once who had strong opinions on almost everything. She was against the whole world, with particular hatred for large companies and successful business people. Someone had said to me that we were made for one another because we were very similar. I wasn't really sure what this meant. We went out one day and spent hours walking around the West End of London. She told me about her parents and grandparents. Politically, they were left-wing, and so she also became left-wing. And that, she said, was something that would never change, even in the smallest way.

As time passed I could see we were not a match made in heaven. Sure we had some similar beliefs, but I just did not believe you can go through life without questioning things. And yet I was listening to someone who believed that her ideas were fully a part of her, as if they had somehow passed by her brain and she had no choice. I hated the idea of taking the second-hand ideas of a particular class or social group and running with them. I had seen the dangers of it. Many years earlier, I had done it myself.

Think, before you believe

Angus was an art student I knew. We would go to exhibitions together and I really liked him. One day as we walked around talking about life, I told him I believed that black people had smaller brains than whites. I actually said that blacks would only ever be good for music and manual labour. He was shocked and upset that I could come out with something like this, and turned on me with such bitterness that I was totally thrown. Honestly, I had no idea what I'd done wrong—I had never before met anybody who had disagreed with me. And here was Angus having a go at me, and I couldn't understand it. Needless to say, our friendship took a huge nosedive after that and, eventually, Angus refused to return my phone calls.

When I had thought about it all for

a while, I asked myself where that idea had come from and who had put it in my head. It certainly wasn't based on experience since I didn't know enough black people to be able to decide whether they were less bright than white people or not. I soon realised it had come from a friend of mine who I thought was a scholar. He acted like he knew everything and seemed to have read lots of books. I suppose I was impressed by his knowledge so I thought he must be right.

That was a lesson in how you can form an opinion on something without ever having given it any proper thought. Yet how many times does this happen? At its most dangerous it can lead to the sort of views expressed by racist and terrorist groups. In everyday terms it casts you as somebody who cannot form your own opinions. Of course, this is no problem if you like hanging around with other people who don't think for themselves. But if you want to progress in your life, that's not going to get you very far.

Give your own true opinion, even if it's different

Have you ever thought why you fear speaking up? Is it because you don't want to look stupid or you are afraid of being mocked? Maybe you don't speak up when your co-workers tell racist jokes because you don't want to rock the boat, even though you think it's wrong. Maybe you go along with your friends' views because you don't want to appear to be 'politically correct'.

There are lots of reasons why we don't say what we really think. And much of it comes down to confidence. You need to feel strong enough to give another view when others all appear to have the same one. And you are only going to do that if you build up your knowledge.

Although I never went very far in school, I have read a lot. In fact, I still read pretty much anything I can get my hands on. And I don't only read about what I agree with. I read work by people who make me so angry I want to throttle them. But I read it because they give me another side of the argument to think about. And because I read a lot, if someone in the pub says something I think is a load of rubbish, I feel confident enough to say something I know they won't agree with. And you know what? Even though people might disagree with me, they respect the fact that I have my own ideas. That is generally the way of things.

Look at Maggie Thatcher, who was in power from 1979 to 1990. During that time she made several decisions that made her unpopular: from removing free milk from schools to introducing the Poll Tax and leading Britain to war over the Falkland Islands. How many people hated what she did in her time as Prime Minister but said that they admired her because she was 'her own person'? She had her convictions and she stuck to them, whether you liked her or not. She is a strong lady.

I have met women who are often too scared to disagree with their partner's opinions. (I'm sure there are men who are the same but I've met more women who are like this.) They let their partner make all the important decisions and accept their opinion because they want to keep the peace. They are always putting themselves second.

I was driving a young woman I knew to the station. She got into the car and I noticed she hadn't put on her seatbelt. Although at the time it wasn't illegal to travel without a seatbelt, I asked her to put it on. 'I don't believe in seatbelts,' she said without a thought. 'It's safer,' I said. But she wouldn't listen. She was a young mother, responsible not only for herself but for her child, who was just a few months old. I tried to convince her but she wouldn't listen.

It turned out that she was just doing what her boyfriend did. He was a very strong personality. And I could imagine him working on this weak young woman who really did not have a mind of her own. His opinions became hers. As well as lacking confidence, she had no sense of her own self-worth. She clearly felt that she did not have any point of view worth offering. As a result it was easy for him to put pressure on her.

Again, it comes back to confidence. Are you the one at work who speaks up in meetings, or the one who leaves thinking, 'I wish I could do that'? If you don't feel happy about speaking up, then you'll like what is coming next. I'm going to tell you a little secret that lots of business people, politicians and others know—that what other people notice most is how you look and sound, and only a tiny part is what you *actually say*. People are far more interested in things like how you stand, move and are dressed, your tone of voice, whether you have any sort of accent, how quickly or slowly you speak, and how easy it is to understand what you are saying. So remember another person is more likely to be swayed by how confident you look and sound than by the actual words you use. Of course, if you have something really worth saying as well, then you are on to a real winner.

Listen to others, but believe in your own ideas

When I started *The Big Issue* there were always people around to tell you how it was. They were experts on the homeless. They said that you shouldn't give homeless people the chance to make their own money because they would spend it unwisely. They never thought that homeless people were used to handouts, and that earning money for themselves freed them from this. I remember being told that I couldn't change anything, and that it would always be like this. My position was simple—that may be the way human beings are, but I didn't agree that things couldn't be made better.

For a short period of time I was seen as a saint. I wasn't trying to be a saint. I was just trying to think for myself. And I proved that you can take a homeless person and help them to develop and become responsible for themselves.

I'm not saying you shouldn't listen to other people. You should. But you should also learn to question them. Look below the surface of things. If you are trying to decide between jobs, for example, get away from other people. Make a list of why you should stay in your current job. Then make a list of why you should move. Cross off the things that matter least until you come to the one or two most important factors on each side. This should help you get pretty close to your decision.

If I had followed the beliefs laid down by my parents and grandparents, then I would never have married a woman whose family came from north-west India. I would never have brought Jewish and black people into my circle of friends. I would never have employed anyone who looked and sounded as though they had come from a totally different culture. I would have hung out with whites and people who hated all foreigners. And I would have not got above myself. I would have made sure that I worked on a building site, or taken up some other suitable job for working men.

*　　　*　　　*

Do you have a dream you want to follow? Are other people giving you their views on your life? You have to take hold of *your* ideas. You have to own them. You have to believe in them, at least until you realise that you don't any longer. And when this happens, you must change them. You have to stop relying on the wisdom of others to form your opinions. You are not a child. You are an adult who has the freedom to think and act for yourself.

- You are not your parents. Respect their views but don't be afraid to form your own.
- Know what your values are and stick to them. If you know what you stand for and you live by it, then others can't pressure you as easily.
- Don't be afraid of people who 'talk the talk'. Remember they are as scared of being found out as you are.

- Your views can change. But they should not change every day, otherwise nobody will believe you.
- Don't be afraid to question others. But first make sure you get things right in your own head.
- Finally remember that confidence is really a big trick that everyone's playing on everyone else.

6 THE IMPORTANCE OF MAKING MISTAKES

If life came with the option of a guarantee, would you buy it? This guarantee would promise that as long as you lived according to certain strict rules, nothing would go wrong. If that meant that you could never take risks or feel the highs and lows of what it means to be human, would you still want it? There would be no despair but there would be no joy either.

Where is it written that life is meant to be a purely rosy journey? I know somebody who feels that if she and her husband argue, their marriage is a total write-off. That's like saying if the car needs cleaning, you should get a new car. These days we make a lot of unreasonable demands on our lives—on ourselves, our children and, yes, our doctors, politicians and business people. We've got to a point where we are terrified of making mistakes. And we don't accept that others should make any either. Worst of all, we wait and almost hope for people to make mistakes, so that we can point a finger at them.

Following the London terrorist bombings last year, the reaction of the emergency services was definitely very fast. Yet there were journalists asking survivors nasty, niggly questions like, 'Do you think they could have been quicker?' And so many people in the USA are afraid of making a mistake and being sued, that they won't stop and help others in the street who may be ill or injured. I know that's an extreme example, but it just shows you how afraid people have become of doing the wrong thing. There are even kids in this country, terrified of failing exams, who have tried to kill themselves.

Whatever happened to being human and the idea that nobody's perfect? Personally I think it is bloody arrogant of anyone to think that nobody else has the right to make mistakes. The fact is that life is all trial and error. Some errors are worse than others. But that's just the way it is. Making mistakes is a vital part of your growth as a person. Without mistakes you don't have anything to learn from. Without mistakes you have no history. Without mistakes you wouldn't know how to do something properly.

There were no blueprints when I started *The Big Issue*. No one had ever worked with homeless people the way we wanted to. No one had ever come up with the mad idea of starting a magazine and hiring the most unreliable workforce on the face of the earth. Against all the wisdom, I did. And I got my fingers burned quite a few times. Not because I was stupid, but because that's just the way life is—not perfect.

Some you lose
In the early days of *The Big Issue* there was a bloke who really impressed me. He was homeless and lived in a tent in Lincolns Inn Fields in London. The Fields had the largest homeless camp in London. This bloke—I'll call him Arthur—came to us with a great idea. He would organise the selling of the papers to the homeless and make sure they didn't rip us off. He seemed careful and did everything he said he would do. So he became our main distributor. Very soon he had people organised so well that our sales rose and kept rising. After about six months you could tell he had everything sorted. He ran our big centre in Victoria and did all the paperwork. He banked all the money and our finance department seemed very happy.

It might be because I was once an offender that I am always slightly suspicious of things that are going too well. One day I asked my finance department to do a spot check of the safe at the distribution office. The finance people were a bit too trusting. They wanted to ring up and tell Arthur that they were coming. I insisted that it had to be a surprise spot check, not planned. Later, the bookkeeper came in to see me. She had gone for the money, but the safe was empty because the safe lock wasn't working too well. So the money had been placed in the pub next door, and the manager of the pub was away. I didn't believe it. I was angry with the bookkeeper and told her there would have to be another spot check. Two days later they checked again. Arthur had gone. So had £11,000.

It was one of our first big lessons and it taught us to think about where problems might occur. We learned not to put temptation in the path of a homeless person who might not have the strength to resist it. We tightened up our system so that it wasn't open to abuse. After that I learned never to expect too much from homeless people. But we did not learn everything we needed to know at once; we kept on learning.

We used to give credit to homeless people if they convinced us that they had some desperate need. The way the system worked was that we gave them their first *Big Issue* bundles free. But after that they had to pay for them up front. Giving credit to mixed-up, troubled people who live on the street was one of the most stupid ideas I have ever been involved in. They never paid us back. They just disappeared so that we lost them and lost the chance to improve their lives. But if we had got it right first time then we would not have been alert for further mistakes. And we would have been open to even bigger rip-offs.

Maybe next year . . .
I am always meeting people who are waiting for the perfect conditions in order to get started. They look upon life as a shit or bust operation. For instance, I have a friend who one day will finish the book he has been working on for 20 years. But it won't be yet. That is because he is always adding more to it. I've listened for years and years to the reasons why the book is not being published that year. The real reason is that he doesn't want to make mistakes. He wants it to be perfect. So it will never happen. If you look at the first copy of *The Big Issue*, it is rubbish compared to what it has become. It was done very quickly. I didn't want to wait until everything was right. I didn't want it to be the best magazine in the world. If I had, I would still be waiting to launch it.

It's smart to think before you act.

There are times I wish I had done so. But if you refuse to act because you are scared of making a mistake, that's a mistake in itself. Refusing to act until you know enough is wise, but refusing to act until you know *everything* makes it a non-starter. Many people lose money on the stock market because they buy without knowing enough. But there are no guarantees on how the market will behave, so if we don't act until we have ALL the information, we will never act. Accept that working out what to do in life is risky anyway, and that you will not make the perfect choice every time. Then your life will be easier.

What are you afraid of?
What's the worst thing that could happen to you as a result of taking that step? Fear of making mistakes is enough to stop us taking risks that could result in making our lives better and more interesting. At the

same time fear also stops us from doing the kind of stupid, reckless things that get us injured, killed or banged up in jail (except for some of us . . .)

The thing you need to work out is which fears are useful and which ones are holding you back. A woman I know tells of her constant, stupid battle with learning to dive from the side of a pool. She can picture herself doing the perfect dive, but she can't bring herself to actually try it. Throughout her life, lots of people have tried to teach her and encourage her, but she still finds herself standing there worrying when she should just be giving it a go. She watches the kids running along the side of the pool and diving in without a second thought, and wishes she could have as much fun as them. She knows the worst thing that could happen is that she belly-flops, but she still can't manage it.

As adults we think far too much

about what could go wrong instead of what could go right. And we end up with something worse than fear—regret. From the regret of not asking for someone's phone number after a really good chat to the regret of not having the courage to leave a job, nothing is worse than being the person who says, 'I wish I had done that.' But you can do something to stop that now. All you need to do is think about yourself in 30, 40 or 50 years' time. Think about telling your grandchildren about your life and the things you did. Now think about the thing you would most regret not doing. It might be taking a journey on your own or going back to study. How would you feel if you could sit there and know that you did it? Pretty good, I would say.

At this point you might think, 'Yeah, good one John, but what if you keep making the same mistakes?' This is like the man or woman who says, 'I know this relationship won't work out because every time I meet somebody it turns out badly.' Have you ever thought why that is? Why do some people always attract the partner who is overbearing, weak or looking for a mother/father figure? It might be because they are not taking the time to learn from their mistakes. They have created a pattern. And the only way to break it is to learn from it. You might think the best thing to do in situations like this is try to forget your mistakes as quickly as you can. But the best thing you can do is think about your mistakes and remember every detail. Only then will you learn why you keep making them.

These days, people flock to me because I seem to be very sure of myself. Homeless people, MPs and police officers all ask me what I think about various things. The fact is that I am no surer of myself than most people are. It is just that I've learned if everything goes tits-up, it's not the end of the world. I don't have to punish myself for my mistakes. And neither do you.

Remember: you only have to start with 3%

Hopefully you have already read the chapter on starting with just 3%. It is about giving yourself targets that you can reach, and then adding to them slowly. Starting with 3% also means you put less pressure on yourself to be perfect. It allows you to move at your own pace. And, yes, it allows you to make mistakes. If you don't try to swallow the whole apple at once then you'll be less likely to choke. And you'll also get more bites at the apple! So you see you don't always have to be right first time.

- Ask yourself what is the worst that can happen. Then ask yourself what is the best that can happen. Chances are the best will cancel out any worries about the worst.

- Don't think you've failed just because you have to change your plans or ideas. The cleverest scientists in the world do that all the time. They don't think of themselves as failures.
- Treasure your mistakes. Don't toss them away. Your successes are only mistakes that have worked, combined with a bit of luck.
- Regret goes deeper than any mistake. When you are old and looking back on your life, what is the thing you would regret not doing? Now go out there and do it.
- Do you want to stay in that dull place? Hop on and enjoy the ride. By taking a chance, you'll meet far more interesting people than if you stay hiding behind your fears.
- Don't wait for things to be perfect before you try. You will

be waiting for ever.
- If I didn't have my mistakes, my cock-ups, and the lessons I learned from them, I wouldn't be writing this today. And my advice would be worthless. So there.

7 BE YOUR OWN LEADER

Being a leader is not about having a title. It is not about being Chairman, Mayor or Team Captain. It is not about having an office the size of a football field and people waiting on you. And it is not about telling people what to do. Leading is not done only by those few in high places, but by you. When you stand up for what you believe in, or act as if what you do matters, then you are leading.

Sian works in a dental surgery. You can tell she is really into her job. She gets in early and gets herself sorted for the day ahead. She looks at the appointment book. And she makes herself aware of the day's work. But you cannot always stick to a timetable so Sian has to balance the time-keeping, the emergencies and the fact that her dentists are not always good at making the best use of their time. She doesn't allow the little things to rattle her. She keeps the show on the road. And the patients who come in know they are going to be well looked after. They also know things are being done in the best way possible. Sian gets everything organised and makes it all work. She does it so well and with such a calm manner that she stands out in the whole of that surgery. Clients come back again and again as much because of her as because of the dentists.

One of the things people notice about Sian is that she doesn't wait to be told what to do. She leads from the front. The way she works sets the tone for the rest of the surgery. Even the dentists follow her lead. That is the mark of a true leader. It isn't about putting on big airs or having people drop to their knees when you come in the room. By showing you have what it takes you will earn the respect of others. You won't get that respect just because you are called Big Boss Poo Bah or whatever.

Take the lead—don't wait for someone else to do it.

There are not enough people like Sian. Instead there are too many people who think it's always up to someone else. I was on the bus with a pram and made my way to the part of the bus reserved for prams. A big fat man with bananas in his hand was standing in the way. He was drunk. I asked him to move aside, which he did, and then he got off the bus, leaving a banana skin behind. I picked it up and put it in the bin, because someone could have slipped on it. I know I am talking real small stuff here. But my point is that every day we take a lead in our own life. Whether we are involved in leading government or business, teaching children, leading a family, standing up for what is right, or organising a dinner, we all have roles as leaders.

Throughout our lives, there will be many roles like this. Some we will know about beforehand, while at other times we will be called upon when we don't expect it. It's up to us to decide whether to take up the challenge or not.

I have always chosen to take the lead when I have had the chance. I have done it also because others did not or could not. Once I was in a group of boys from the youth institution where I lived. In a bid to make us tougher (the right kind of tough) they took us out and dropped us in open country with a map and enough water for the day. Our job was to return to base camp. There we were, six unruly troublemakers in the middle of the countryside with no hope of finding a road sign or a friendly stranger.

None of us knew how to read a map and we had no idea where to find north, south, east or west. So we just kept on walking and walking. We had a leader. Well, sort of. He was the most senior boy so everyone thought he had it in him to lead. But as we all got hot and hungry, he didn't have a clue what to do. Nobody did. So without saying anything I took over. I went up a hill and looked around. A few miles down the road I could see some houses. I came back and told the other boys we were going to walk towards them.

We finally got to the town houses. As we were hungry I knocked on one of the doors. A woman opened it. I told her that our supplies had been washed away in the river and asked for some bread. The woman took us in and showed us to her garden. She made tea and sandwiches, boiled eggs for us and fed us royally. If she had known we were a bunch of nasty kids from the slums of London she might have had other thoughts. But I made sure I did all the talking. And I took charge of the boys when we went in. I told them they could not steal anything and had to behave in the best possible way. When we had finished, I thanked the lady and led our motley little group out to the road again in single file, as though we were the best boy scouts in the world.

Times when someone has to take charge

In some ways my childhood forced me to become a leader. Those of you who have had tough childhoods may know what I mean. You have to develop a sense of responsibility because otherwise you will sink. When I was very young, we were made homeless. We moved into a room without windows in the loft of my grandmother's house. Three boys in a bed at one end with my mother and father at the other end. Every Friday and Saturday night my mother and father would go out to the pub for a drink. They got very drunk. Then they came home and fought in the alley below the window of my grandmother's house. Where I came from, it was quite common for the wife to be beaten. That is exactly what my father did to my mother down in the alley.

My two elder brothers would cry and whimper, as if it was they who were being beaten. Aged seven and eight, they were very scared of the sound of my father laying into my mother. I would comfort them. I would not cry. I would not share their fear. At that time, something stopped me from becoming a beaten animal like them, but later I became one myself. I feared my father so much that all my bad dreams were about being beaten and killed by my father. Even now, long after his death, I have a fear that comes back to me at night. It is the fear of this madman hurting me and my mother. But in the middle of it all I took the lead with my elder brothers. I would not let this horrible thing control me.

True leaders are often found at the worst of times. During the tsunami that hit Asia on Boxing Day in 2004, people who were on holiday gave help where it was needed. They didn't wait to be asked. They just looked at things and made up their minds what had to be done. Then they just got on with it. Other leaders appeared during the London bombings in 2005. They were members of the public who just took the lead and did what they thought needed to be done.

A couple of years ago I watched a TV programme about people who were awarded the Victoria Cross medal for extreme courage at war. Winning the Victoria Cross is a very hard thing to do. For one thing, you need to have faced death. You also need to have shown leadership at the very worst times. The winners had all done that. There is no question they were heroes. But what was really interesting about them is that they seemed very ordinary and modest, and not the kind of people who talked or acted big. They were ordinary soldiers who didn't go into the war as big leaders. Some had commanding roles, but others were simple men from the infantry.

When they were called upon to do their duty, they did so with something special that very few of us can match. They knew they had a job to do and, by God, they were going to do it to the utmost. The desire to fight for their country and to protect their men was all they thought about. For me they showed leadership at its very best. Yet, as the programme showed, not one of them thought they were doing anything special. They said they were just doing their jobs.

Leaders can be doing the most ordinary things (but it's how they do it).

A lot of stuff is written about how to be a great leader. In fact there are hundreds and hundreds of books—and most of them are rubbish. They don't end up helping you. All they do is remind you that you are not up there. And they see leading as something that is big, very big. They see it as something you do if you want to be a Prime Minister, or a billionaire like Bill Gates—founder of the giant computer software company Microsoft, and said to be worth around $40 billion. We don't need any more big chiefs in this world. We need more everyday leaders who will change the world for the better—like Sian.

What about the man who sweeps the street in front of my house? You might think he has a crummy job, but it is his way of helping the world go round. I've watched him through the window. He does his job with great pride, making sure that the footpath is clean and that any weeds growing out of the cracks in the concrete are pulled up. I'm not sure if he has to do all that, but he does it anyway. His attitude shows he is a leader. He is committed to the job. He takes control. And he does it properly. He understands the value of starting with 3%. He knows that big things come from small things.

There are many people who do not want to take the lead in life. They think it's always for someone else to take on. They are the ones who say, 'That's not my job.' These people want to be paid more or given some other reward before they will change and act in a different way. That's the wrong way to be. You have to show you are a leader by doing the job or task first. You need to do this so people can see what you are made of. If you are the sort of person who always thinks it's not your job, then it's likely that you don't have what it takes.

Not wanting to lead doesn't give you the right to knock people who do. I have talked about why knocking people is not a good idea earlier in this book. And there's nothing worse than people who won't take the lead, attacking those who do. If you don't want to speak up, if you don't want to put up, then please shut up. Don't be that someone who whinges about others but won't lift a finger or make their voice heard except to back-stab people.

Real leaders show their true colours in every aspect of their life. Their vision of a better world doesn't just apply to their job. They put it into action when they pick up litter, or stop to help people who are lost, or ask people to move up on the bus so that others will be more comfortable. They are always thinking about others as well as themselves. They may be ambitious individuals but they are also unselfish in many ways. And they have strong values. They know what they believe in and are able to think for themselves. This means they have less trouble making decisions, which is very important, whether you are leading yourself through life or looking after others. Being your own leader is knowing that the things you do can help to make a better world for yourself as well as others.

- Leading is taking pride in the things that you do.
- Leading is about doing what needs to be done before you are told.
- Leaders don't choose only the best bits of anything. They do it all.
- Leaders take responsibility for themselves and the world around them. They believe they can make a difference.
- Leaders don't need to talk or act big. It is enough just being who they are.

- Leaders don't knock others—they support them.
- Leaders never say, 'It isn't my job.'

Conclusion

Andy came up to me with a smile and shook my hand. 'John, I've kicked it. I'm in control, pal.'

'Really?' I stood up near him and looked closer at him. I could smell drink on his breath.

'Yes, John.'

'But I can still smell the drink on you.'

He smiled again. 'From 15 cans and a bottle of vodka a day to two cans after work is something to be proud of.'

I had to laugh. He was right. He had not done all he wanted. He was looking forward to the day when he could walk past a pub and not want to go in. He hadn't got there yet but he was very pleased with himself. A few years later he gave up drink for good. But that night he was just happy that he had turned a bad habit into something a bit more social.

Andy knew how to feel good about what he had done. We all need to do that. No matter how small that 3% is, you need to enjoy your achievements. Even if what you have done is so small that others don't notice, it doesn't matter. At this point in my life I still take joy in my small steps. Recently that has meant discovering the joys of being neat and tidy. For most of my life I ignored the mess I made. Last year I got married and now I can see the joy in being organised. I don't expect you to get excited about the fact that I like knowing I have put the rubbish out on time. It is my little step. And that is how you should think about your own life.

If you have read this book and like what you hear, then you have a lot of big days to look forward to:

- The day you decide to start with 3%.
- The day you stop feeling sorry for yourself and blaming the world for your problems.
- The day you stop hanging on to lies and excuses.
- The day you stop knocking other people.
- The day you start using your own mind and developing your own opinions.
- The day you feel free to make mistakes.
- The day you decide to be your own leader.

Some people who find success tell me it's not all it's cracked up to be. To me that sounds like the wrong kind of success. True success is when you feel fulfilled. It may not come from only one part of your life; it may be a combination of things. Looking at what I have done, I would say success for me means one thing. And it isn't *The Big Issue*. It's the fact that I didn't follow in my father's footsteps. I didn't react to the difficult things in life like he did, by beating up a woman. When I feel down I take great comfort and pride in that. All the other things that I have like authority, respect and power mean nothing beside the feeling that I have achieved greatness in my own small way.

I hope you find your own small piece of greatness. Good Luck.

John Bird